Ransom Neutron Stars
Curry!
by Cath Jones

Published by Ransom Publishing Ltd.
Unit 7, Brocklands Farm, West Meon, Hampshire GU32 1JN, UK
www.ransom.co.uk

ISBN   978 178591 435 5
First published in 2017

Curry!

Cath Jones

Ransom

This is oil.

5

This is in the pan.

This is an onion.

Tip the onion
in the pan.

This is a chilli.

Tip the chilli
in the pan.

This is a carrot.

17

Tip the carrot
in the pan.

This is garlic.

Tip the garlic in the pan.

This is ginger.

Tip the ginger
in the pan.

This is chicken.

Tip the chicken
in the pan.

This is a tomato.

Tip the tomato
in the pan.

This is water.

Tip the water
in the pan.

This is curry.
Yum!

Have you read?

Free Runners

by
Alice Hemming

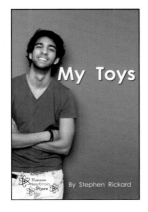

My Toys

by
Stephen Rickard

Ransom Neutron Stars

Curry!
Word count **88**

Pink Book Band

Phonics

Phonics 1	Not Pop, Not Rock Go to the Laptop Man Gus and the Tin of Ham	*Phonics 2*	Deep in the Dark Woods Night Combat Ben's Jerk Chicken Van
Phonics 3	GBH Steel Pan Traffic Jam Platform 7	*Phonics 4*	The Rock Show Gaps in the Brain New Kinds of Energy

Book bands

Pink	**Curry!** Free Runners My Toys	*Red*	Shopping with Zombies Into the Scanner Planting My Garden
Yellow	Fit for Love The Lottery Ticket In the Stars	*Blue*	Awesome ATAs Wolves The Giant Jigsaw
Green	Fly, May FLY! How to Start Your Own Crazy Cult The Care Home	*Orange*	Text Me The Last Soldier Best Friends